BREAK THROUGH

YOU CAN BEAT THE ODDS

SHAKISHA EDNESS

BREAKTHROUGH Volume I

Published by T.R.A.C Publishing

Cover design: Jacobie Brown

Editor: Shanice Edness

Cover illustration: Google

Interior illustration: Google

Interior design: T.R.A.C Publishing

Bible Scriptures: New Living Translation

Printed in the United States of America.

ISBN- 10: 0692255109

ISBN-13: 978-0692255100

DEDICATION

THIS BOOK IS DEDICATED TO WOMEN

I thank you for purchasing this book and sowing a seed into my life as I am being used, by God, to sow a seed into yours.

I wrote two books titled *BREAK THROUGH*. One book speaks directly to women and the other is designed for men.

When God initially spoke to me about this book, it was created just for men. As God began giving me revelation for both partners, I was excited to have a word for women as well. I am honored to be used by God.

Please buy *Break Through Volume II* for your fiancé or husband, because it will ignite the fire into the relationship and the fire will burn forevermore.

Blessings and Miracles...

A personal special dedication to the following women in my life, that I want to see God allow a Break Through to take place in their lives individually, collectively, and generationally.

Rhoda Aleaxander, "Thank you for always, and I do mean always, having my back. God has truly used you as a form of my Break Through for my life. This is dedicated to you grandma, thanks for everything!" **Supporter...**

Shahidah Edness, "Never think you're invisible. I see every ounce of your growth and I know that God has a Break Through that is tailored made for you." **Persevere**...

Shukriyyah Edness, "You are truly extraordinary, in every way. You have a gift that won't ever allow you to be stuck. That gift is having Faith and Believing that all things are possible. Get your Break Through today!" ***Believer...***

Shanice Edness, "You helped me deliver my babies, you encouraged me to push, and yet you was still sensitive to my emotions. I thank you. I truly cannot find the words to express the Joy that I have, as a result of your help. Bless you richly." ***Midwife...***

Annisha James Walton, "You have given me every reason to trust God and to not give up, because that's exactly what I hear when I hear your voice. Never underestimate the Power of the Holy Spirit, He uses you more than you know. I love you not like a sister, but as my sister." ***Endurer...***

Tranisha Hollman, "You have truly inspired me along my journey in everything and in every way. I have cried and prayed. And you always reminded me that I can do it! Thank you for believing in me. I love you Beautiful!" ***Cheerleader...***

Cassandra Hollman, "You have prayed with me and for me. We have rejoiced with one another, fought with one another, and been there for one another regardless. I thank and love you. Break Through NOW!" ***Soldier...***

Shandra Small, "You let me be me! You do not expect me to be anyone else other than myself. With that said, you have blessed me in such a way that no one has and I thank you. I love you just the way you are! You keep it real and that's what I love about you, because you leave me no room but to do the same." ***Authentic...***

Kate Terrell, "You are truly my Spiritual Mother and it's just that simple, I love you dearly." ***Naomi...***

CONTENTS

Acknowledgments

1   Story of Judah and Tamar   13

2   Tamar's Teachings   25

3   The Twelve Steps of Tamar   29

4   Judah's Lessons   39

5   A Word From The Lord   45

6   In My Own Words   49

7   Scriptures Just For You   55

About The Author

ACKNOWLEDGMENTS

I thank God for allowing me to read His word and allowing His word to come alive in me like never before. Therefore, enabling me to release it to His people and watch Him do as He said. I thank Him for speaking to me, through me, and for me. This is a story that I read that truly blessed me in a way that I will forever be thankful to God.

I sincerely and wholeheartedly thank my daughter and editor, Shanice Edness for the time sown into editing my books (eight to ten hours at a time). You cannot imagine how much I appreciate you. Many turned me away, because I could not financially afford them. Others rejected me, because they did not believe in my dream. A few individuals thought I was their competition. But God! He sent someone that could afford to be a blessing to someone else. And not take the credit, but give Him the Glory that belongs to Him. May every seed sown boomerang back into your life one thousand fold.

Jacobie Brown, my graphic designer, friend, and whom I call my son. You are truly a blessing in disguise. I cannot find the words to express how great you have been to me. You have been up with me in the late night hours, working on projects when you knew I had nothing to give in return. You constantly said, "Momma, no worries. I am sowing seed." I pray God opens His floodgates, breaking every barrier, allowing the seeds sown to spring forth a harvest that you won't have room enough to receive.

I thank many for praying for me, believing in me, and supporting me.

Reginald Leonard, "Thank you for always calling and standing in the gap for me by constantly praying with me and for me."

Adrian Manning, "The way God has spoken through you during this process, has truly kept me focused and helped me to refocus."

Also, I would like to give thanks to a man that I love dearly. I can still remember when I called him and asked him if he had previously said there was a man midwife in the bible. He responded, "No." I then asked, "Well, what did you say your middle name was?" He said, "Perez." I asked, "What does it mean?" He said, "Break Through. Read Gen 38:28-30."

The funny thing is that I was already reading Genesis 38, but I was at the beginning of the story. I had not yet made it to the end. So when he directed me to that story, I made sure I read the entire story. I marveled, because instantly God spoke to me announcing, *"BREAK THROUGH!"*

On May 18, 2013, my birthday, I attended this man's graduation. He was a country boy from Alabama and the ninth child born of his siblings.

He is the first of all to graduate in his family. He attended the military service, moved to Atlanta, and continued his education in college at Strayer University in Douglasville, Georgia. This man was determined to break through the barriers, obstacles, excuses, and the generational curses in order to tap into the generational blessings for himself, his family, and the generations to come.

He has a career, a home, a car, and most of all a relationship with Christ.

His testimony spoke to my life and it is part of the reason for this book being written as well. He has been a blessing to me and has silently encouraged me to pursue my dreams as an Author.

Blessings O.P.B.

God used him to help me deliver what was in me; this is my *Break Through!*

INTRODUCTION

Are you praying for a breakthrough? Have you heard the pastor or the prophet say that a breakthrough was coming your way? Have you yet received it?

Have you been told you are barren? Did the doctor say that you will never be able to birth children of your own? Do you believe God can speak life into your womb and allow a baby to come forth? You do? Amen, keep reading.

Does your husband complain that you are lazy. Does he complain that you do not cook or clean and you barely give him sex? Does this sound familiar?

What is barren?

Barren is incapable of reproducing; unproductive. To reproduce is to copy or duplicate; to propagate. Propagate is to breed or multiply; to spread or extend.

Has the Man of God planted something into you, for you to birth out? Has He given you something to work on lately? Is He planting on fertile ground?

This does not necessarily mean a baby, but may be His vision or dream. Has He shared His vision with you?

Be honest with yourself. After seeing the cover of this book and reading the synopsis, if it speaks directly to you I encourage you to invest in yourself by purchasing it.

What if the breakthrough you are waiting on, is waiting on you to
BREAK THROUGH!

1

The Story of Judah & Tamar

About this time, Judah left home and moved to Adullam, where he visited a man named Hirah. 2There he met a Canaanite woman, the daughter of Shua, and he married her. 3She became pregnant and had a son, and Judah named the boy Er. 4Then Judah's wife had another son, and she named him Onan. 5And when she had a third son, she named him Shelah. At the time of Shelah's birth, they were living at Kezib. 6When his oldest son, Er, grew up, Judah arranged his marriage to a young woman named Tamar. *7But Er was a wicked man in the Lord's sight, so the Lord took his life.*

Er was a wicked man in the sight of the Lord, so the Lord took his life.

This lets me know that we must be concerned about how God views us; not how man views us.

Woman of God, is your husband a wicked man in God's sight?

8Judah said to Er's brother Onan "You must marry Tamar, as our law requires of the brother of a man who has died. Her first son from you will be your brother's heir." 9But Onan was not willing to have a child who would not be his own heir. So whenever he had intercourse with Tamar he spilled the semen on the ground to keep her from having a baby who would belong to his brother. 10But the Lord considerate it a wicked thing for Onan to deny a child to his dead brother. So the Lord took Onan's life, too.

Onan was told to marry Tamar and get her pregnant. Giving his brother an heir, who would be the first born son. But Onan disobeyed by having intercourse with Tamar and spilling the semen on the ground, keeping her from getting pregnant. He refused to give his deceased brother a living heir.

And the Lord considered this to be a wicked thing, for Onan to deny a child to his dead brother. So the Lord took Onan's life as well.

Er lost his life because he was wicked and evil. Then, Onan lost his life because he committed wickedness in the sight of God. One brother was evil and the other did evil things. Both killed by God!

Woman of God, is your husband doing wicked things and being disobedient in the sight of God?

We are always concerned about what others will say or how they look at us. But it's time for us to start being concerned with what the Lord considers evil and how He views us.

11Then Judah told Tamar, his daughter – in – law; not to marry again at this time but to return to her parents' home. She was to remain a widow until his youngest son, Shelah, was old enough to marry her. (But Judah did not really intend to do this because he was afraid Shelah would also die like his two brothers). So Tamar went home to her parents.

Do your in-laws blame you, because your husband is dead? You are not the problem!

Being dead does not mean it has to be a physical death. It can be a spiritual, mental, emotional, and/or financial death. A person can be socially dead as well.

Er and Onan are both deceased now and Tamar is still not pregnant. She was instructed by Judah (her father – in – law) to go home with her parents and stay a widow until Shelah gets old enough to marry her. Although, knowing he had no intentions on giving his son to her, because he was afraid that he would also die. But she was unaware, so she did as she was told.

12In the course of time Judah's wife died. After the time of mourning was over, Judah and his friend Hirah the Adullamite went to Timnah to supervise the shearing of his sheep. <u>13Someone told Tamar that her father – in – law had left for the sheep – shearing at Timnah. 14Tamar was aware that Shelah had grown up. But they had not called her to marry him.</u>

The word gets around!

Tamar is aware that Shelah was old enough to marry, but they had not yet arranged for them to marry.

Say out loud, "Tamar takes matters into her own hands!" You and I both know that the worse thing a man can do to a woman, is break his promise to her and having her wait while making a fool of her! That's a word right there ladies!

<u>So she changed out of her widow's clothing and covered herself with a veil to disguise herself. Then she sat along the road at the entrance to the village of Enaim, which is on the way to Timnah.</u>

Tamar disguised and covered herself with a veil and sat beside the road at the entrance to the village of Enaim, that is on the way to Timnah.

Basically, she set up a plan to deceive Judah. She was in a place that he would pass her by.

15Judah noticed her as he went by and thought she was a prostitute, since her face was veiled. 16So he stopped and propositioned her to sleep with him, not realizing that she was his own daughter – in – law.

He is biting the bait ladies! He was unaware of her being his daughter - in - law and propositioned her for sexual relations. His wife was deceased and he was in need of sex.

"How much will you pay me?" Tamar asked. "I will send you a young goat from my flock," Judah promised. "What pledge will you give me so I can be sure you will send it?" she asked. "Well what do you want?" he inquired. She replied, "I want your identification seal, your cord, and the walking stick you are carrying."

Negotiation began.

So Judah gave these items to her. She then let him sleep with her, and she became pregnant. 19Afterwards, she went home, took off her veil, and put on her widow's clothing as usual.

She negotiated with Judah and she got what she requested as collateral. She proceeded to meet his need, after she was secured. Sounds like a business transaction to me.

Mission accomplished!

20Judah asked his friend Hirah the Adullamite to take the young goat back to her and to pick up the pledges he had given her, but Hirah couldn't find her. 21So he asked the men who lived there, "Where can I find the prostitute who was sitting beside the road at the entrance to the village?"

Judah is trying to make good on his promise, by sending his friend to deliver the promise and pick up his pledges. Have the man of God kept his promise to you lately? His word should be his bond!

But it's strange how Judah will keep his promise to a stranger, or shall I say a prostitute, but not his daughter - in - law.

Please make note of this! A man cannot choose when or who he decides to keep his word to, he should always be a man of his word.

His friend, Hirah, was a true friend because he tried to find her at all cost.

Does your husband have a close friend? A man needs a friend other than you. So please allow him to have one without you feeling intimidated or not trusting him. So many men do not go out with their friends, because they are being held accountable for the last man that may have cheated on his current spouse.

"We've never had a prostitute here." They replied. 22So Hirah returned to Judah and told him that he couldn't find her anywhere and that the men of the village had claimed they didn't have a prostitute there. 23"Then let her keep the pledges!" Judah exclaimed. "We tried our best to send her the goat. We'd be the laughingstock of the village if we went back again."

Judah knew he had a reputation to live up to, like many men today. So he was not willing to jeopardize it. I must admit, he tried to keep his promise. Is your husband living up to his godly or worldly reputation?

24About three months later, word reached Judah that Tamar, his daughter – in – law was pregnant as a result of prostitution. "Bring her out and burn her!" Judah shouted. 25But as they were taking her out to kill her, she sent this message to her father – in – law: "The man who owns this identification seal and walking stick is the father of my child. Do you recognize them?"

Okay let's pause for a second. Three months later, word reached Judah that Tamar was pregnant as a result of prostitution. The word got out often around there!

Judah was furious with Tamar for bringing shame on him and his family, by being pregnant as a result of prostitution! He instructed them to bring her out and burn her! Meaning he is going to kill her publicly, in front of everyone!

As they took her out to kill her, she pulled out her ammunition! Her ammunition was what she negotiated three months prior, which was what Judah gave her as collateral. He gave her his identification seal, cord, and walking stick.

I am sure Tamar was scared to death, but she dealt the hand and now she had to play her hand carefully.

She had everything to lose and even more to gain. Her life was at risk, along with her unborn child.

Woman of God, where is your ammunition? What is it, that you have everything to lose but even more to gain?

Judah do you recognize them?

26Judah admitted that they were his and said, "She is more in the right than I am, because I didn't keep my promise to let her marry my son Shelah." But Judah never slept with Tamar again.

Judah took responsibility of his part and sparred her life. He is an honest man, because he told the truth. He openly admitted that they belonged to him and he accepted that she was pregnant by him. This speaks highly of his character.

I know so many men who lay with women and get them pregnant, but deny that the child is his. In most cases, they even deny they had had ever slept with the mother of the child.

Does your husband admit when he is wrong? Does he take responsibility for the role he played?

Do not let him place the blame on you. He must take ownership as well.

27In due season the time of Tamar's delivery arrived, and she had twin sons.

In due season you shall receive double for your trouble! We hear this regularly from pastors. This has been confirmed.

Tamar was married to two of Judah's sons and she didn't bear a child from either one of them. Then, he denied her his third son.

But she was rewarded with two sons. I think she birthed two sons, representing both husbands, through the seeds of their father. Let's not forget this was a blessing to Judah as well.

28As they were being born, one of them reached out his hand, and the midwife tied the scarlet thread around the wrist of the child who appeared first, saying "This one came out first."

29But then he drew back his hand, and the other baby was actually the first to be born. "What!" the midwife exclaimed. "How did you break out first?" And ever after he was called Perez. 30Then the baby with the scarlet thread on his wrist was born, and he was named Zerah.

One appeared to be delivered first. But as he drew his hand back, the other twin son broke through becoming the first born. He was named Perez! *Perez* meaning *break through*. And the second born was named *Zerah,* which means *arise.*

Now that I have laid the foundation of this message, it is time for me to build the house.

Can I preach this word the way I would if I was standing outside of a liquor store or in the pulpit? It does not matter to me whether I am on my front porch or standing outside the door of the church.

I have preached this word in barbershops and on the telephone. And every time I felt the Holy Spirit move over those men and women like no other. I pray the same anointing falls afresh upon you and this word will come alive in you as well.

Father God, decrease me and increase you! None of me but all of you! God, I ask that your anointing reign down on the Woman of God, that is reading this book right now in Jesus Name Amen!

You may be a woman that has been told you are barren, cannot birth children, or your husband is infertile and cannot produce a child. The doctor gave you this news months or years ago and you believed it.

Though you continue to pray and cry at night begging God to bless your womb, you are not sure it will happen. Why?

Because you have not yet been blessed with a child. Hold your faith and continue to read.

Maybe you are married to a man that has closed his heart and even though you are married, you have yet gotten pregnant. Because he won't release what's in him into you; so you can birth it out.

Can we talk one on one? Well, you cannot talk back but I want you to relax yourself.

Relax is to ease tension or stress, to be or make less stringent or intense.

You are aware that when reading anything it speaks to you where you are, directs you to your next move, and gives you clarity and awareness.

But everyone can read the same thing and get different perspectives. Why is that? Well, I know of two reasons. One, because we have two things that makes us different; our beliefs and experiences.

With those two reasons being brought to the forefront, I ask you to allow yourself to see this from a different perspective. Regardless of our beliefs being different and us having different experiences.

Our experiences and beliefs has such an impact on our lives and the lives of others. We must one day take a look at how they are helping or hurting us.

So let me introduce myself. Hello, I am woman of God after God's own heart. I have been hurt, abandoned, abused mentally, emotionally, and physically by a man I once loved. I was beat with a pistol, spit in my face, and stomped while I was carrying his child. And the year my daughter walked across the stage to get her diploma, he had the audacity to tell me I deserved every bit of it!

I guess you are questioning, what did she do to deserve that? I did not love myself and I allowed him to do everything he did to me.

The reason I am sharing this is because this could have been the very reason I cut men off and decided to never deal with a man again. No, I did not cut them off for life, thank God!

Nevertheless, I did shut them out for six years of my life.

Woman of God, have you closed your womb to receive from the Man of God?

Not to mention, I experienced abandonment first from my father. For years, I was unaware of what abandonment was because I never had him in my everyday life, so it was familiar to me. But I expected something different from him.

Do you expect something different from your husband than what your father gave you?

But should every man pay for what he has done to me? Of course not. It is not fair to me or the man that is ordained to be my husband. So I decided to destroy the wall I built, shutting men out not allowing him in, but not allowing me to come out either. Breaking the wall will help me have who God designed for me. And it will also help me to do His purpose.

This book has been written because women tend to build walls out of steel and cement so men aren't able to reach her; men have done the same thing.

Men are not just using condoms, they are wearing them! Men wear condoms protecting themselves from being hurt or hurt again, rather.

Maybe he was not raised by his mother and/or she abandoned him.

Or his ex-girlfriend broke his heart and his heart never healed. Here is a good one, you may remind him of his mother or ex.

But in reality men are killing themselves, because they are doing the opposite of what God designed them to do. Not to mention, killing the vision that God has placed inside of him. It is designed to be released into a woman (his wife), so that she can nurture and birth it out!

No, he cannot birth out the vision alone! The vision can be a business, ministry, and/or a child. He needs you, Woman of God, in order to birth it!

In order for you to birth out the vision that is in him, he must be willing to release it into you. So if you knew there was a vision in your husband, that will be a blessing to you both, what would you do to get him to release it into you?

Yes, you have work to do.

Open yourself up to receive the Word of God.

Everything that you long for is in God and His Word.

John 1:1 - 5

1In the beginning the Word already existed. He was with God, and he was God. 2He was in the beginning with God. 3He created everything there is. Nothing exists that he didn't make. 4Life itself was in him, and this life gives light to everyone. 5The light shines through the darkness, and the darkness can never extinguish it.

Isaiah 55:11

11It is the same with my word, I send it out, and it will prosper everywhere I send it.

2

The Teachings of Tamar

As I read this story, the Lord began to open my eyes to the message for women. It blessed me in such a way and I pray it does the same for you.

The first thing Tamar did was she obeyed the orders given to her. When her father – in – law instructed her to return to her parents and stay a widow until Shelah gets old enough to marry. By the time Shelah was of age, he would give him to her. With her not being aware that he was not going to keep his word, she obeyed. She trusted him.

Then after she got word he was heading to the sheep – shearing, she knew Shelah was of age to marry but Judah had not kept his promise to her. She took off her widow clothes and dressed in disguise with a veil over her head.

She is hiding her true identity so he will not recognize her.

She sat beside the road at the entrance to the village of Enaim, which is on the way to Timnah. Judah noticed her as he went by and thought she was a prostitute, since her face was concealed.

This message shares a lot. She sat, meaning she patiently waited. And she went where he would see her and come to her.

So he stopped and propositioned her to sleep with him, not realizing that she was his own daughter – in – law. "How much will you pay me?" Tamar asked.

She asked by giving him the lead, not demanding anything. She asked what he was willing to pay her. "I will send you a young goat from my flock," Judah promised.

Woman of God, she was really working her magic. She did not command anything, but she let him say what he can afford and/or what he wanted to give her.

Because many times we as women demand what we want from a man and he is not able or willing to deliver it. She was smart by letting him say what he would do, so he would have no excuse for not doing it. Amen. Let's proceed.

Not to mention, he had already lied to her in the past.

"What pledge will you give me, so I can be sure you will send it?" she asked. "Well what do you want?" he inquired.

This is awesome! Do you see how she has made him comfortable with her, because now he is giving her the lead? I was taught ladies first. But I am learning that in order for us to get what we want, sometimes we should let him go first. Then, it will ease his tension.

Tamar made him comfortable and Judah, in return, gave her room to negotiate with him. See how things are falling into place for her?

She replied, "I want your identification seal, cord, and the walking stick you are carrying." So Judah gave these items to her.

The above items she requested were valuable to him. These were symbols of a man's identity and to whom he is connected to. I mean, think of it like this, she was really asking him for his I.D, social security card, and birth certificate.

Can you imagine asking for a man's state I.D., social security card, and certificate of birth before having sexual relations with him? Then imagine him giving it to you! I have not seen it yet.

 An identification card represents who he is and where he lives. The birth certificate gives information on who he is connected to and where he comes from. And his social security card lets me know his status. Or tells me what he is about.

The birth certificate certifies who his parents are. His social security number (if ran through a credit report system) tells me how much debt he's had or has, his previous addresses, and who he banks with. Do you feel this is valuable information that should be shared? I do!

Seriously, this is telling a lot about him. How many women sleep with a man before knowing who he is, where he's from, who he is connected to, and what he is about? We do not know his credit report, income, or past history; but we lay with him!

And how many men will give you this information?

But Judah gave them to her. Basically, Judah had nothing to hide. This is when she collected the collaterals.

She then let him sleep with her and she became pregnant. It was not until after she collected the pledges, then she allowed his request to be fulfilled. She had to secure the agreement before fulfilling it.

Afterwards she went home, took off her veil, and put on her widow's attire as usual.

She served him and both purposes were accomplished!   She returned home and dressed for business as usual.

He wanted sex and she wanted a baby.

Are you enlightened by what the Word has revealed so far? I am.

I began wondering about the fact that I have been doing the opposite for years. It is time for women to rise to the occasion. Stop doing things the way the world instructs you to and begin doing it the way God tells you.

In the next portion of this book, I will share the learned qualities of Tamar. This is her twelve step program.

3

The Twelve Steps of Tamar

Tamar's twelve steps goes as follows:

1. She obeyed him.
2. She disguised herself.
3. She wore a veil.
4. She waited.
5. She questioned him.
6. She made him comfortable.
7. She negotiated with him.
8. She collected the collaterals from him.
9. She secured the deal with him.
10. She let him sleep with her.
11. The purpose was fulfilled for both of them.
12. Mission was accomplished.

Woman of God allow me to share a little with you. When was the last time you obeyed the Man of God? God's word says obedience is better than sacrifice. So you want to argue with me? What is your argument? "I do obey God," says the Woman of God! And she says it with attitude. Yes, I am laughing out loud.

His word also says submit yourself to your husband. To submit is to obey.

Many women have been single for far too long. And we have done it all by ourselves. Now that a man is the head of our household, it's hard to let him take charge. As for myself, I am still single and the head of my household, but I am preparing myself in this area. How? Glad you asked.

When making decisions, I ask myself questions I think would concern my husband. If I feel he wouldn't want me to do something, I either don't partake of it or I remind myself that that would no longer be an option once I am married.

Queen, it is okay to obey because there is a blessing on the other side of obedience. Remember, obedience is better than what? Sacrifice.

After she obeyed, she disguised herself. Men get tired of seeing the same thing over and over again. Men are visually satisfied. You must do something to catch and keep his attention!

She did not want him to recognize her, because she intended to deceive him. But let me show you the positive side of this. She did not want him to know who she was, but she did want him to see her. You want him to view you differently. The one thing we have in common with Tamar is that we want to be recognized by our men.

Even the veil makes a statement, because to veil your face is covering your identity. Women of God, can I speak to you woman to woman? Thanks for giving me permission.

You must be able to please him and he does not always want to be confronted by the Christian woman. He wants to speak to the freak! He may want to speak to the business woman or someone that can have an intelligent conversation, without the pistol being aimed in his face. Yes, always beating him with the word!

I am not telling you not to be the Christian woman who loves God, but the veil says I am covering that side of me. You must change his perception of you.

He may need advice on business or handling something that requires you to think outside of the box. I hope you understand what I am saying. Many women miss this and lose their man/husband. Yes, he can still be in reach and be lost.

So learn how to cover yourself at the right time and for the right reasons.

She covered and waited. Wait on the Lord and be of good courage. This is a sensitive subject for women. We want what we want, right now!

When I think of Tamar finding out Judah deceived her, I would have handled this much differently than she did. I would have gone to where he was, knocked on the door, and told him to come here because I had a few words for him. I would have cursed him out! Yes, now you can understand why I am alone. Now you're laughing, but that's not funny!

I would have done this openly and publicly, demanding him to give me what he promised. Probably proceeding to hit him or bust a few windows and tires. No, I am kidding, but I did do things of that nature in my past. It did not get me anywhere. It left me single!

Wait on the Man of God to notice you. Trust me he will see what attracts his attention.

Being loud and embarrassing him will not get his attention in a positive manner. It will direct him to leave the situation and that means leaving you!

I hope I am saving someone's marriage or engagement.

When the Man of God approaches you, be prepared to ask questions. Inquire about what he is willing to give you.

"How much will you pay me?" she asked. She is smart. She knew if he wanted his need met, he would be willing to exchange something for it. She discerned that he had something to give. She recognized him but he did not recognize her. Do you have knowledge of the Man of God?

Many women will not ask, because they are afraid that they may not receive it. Others will give it away for free, because they do not want to be looked upon as a "gold digger". And a few will give it, thinking it will get them what they want without them having to ask for it.

Come on and talk back to me, because I am speaking nothing but the truth.

Well, I guess if she wants a baby. NO, just kidding. Keep reading.

How many times were you talking with a friend and during the conversation you were bragging on your man's gifts, then her head dropped? You questioned, "What has her man done for her lately?" Not to mention you know her man has money, but you now realized she is not getting to the money. Okay, now you are with me.

She defends herself by saying that she doesn't want him for his money. No, she is afraid to ask him for his money!

Because a woman asks her man for money, does not suggest money is all she wants! A man wants you to ask him for what you need and/or want.

Maybe she is like most, always saying, I do not need a man to take care of me. See that's a major problem with these Twenty First Century women today. If you do not need a man to take care of you, please tell me what do you want with him?

I am sick of hearing women say, "I want my own job and my own money." For real? Okay, let me share something with you to give you a different outlook on this matter.

To care for is to have concern, act with caution, and having responsibility.

A woman that makes the statement that they do not need a man to take care of her is in turn saying that she does not want him to be concerned or have any responsibility for her. She wants for him to never act with caution, while dealing with her. And women wonder why men show no regards to them.

A man is supposed to take care of his family. A man that obeys God's word does just that. God said, "Love your wife as I love the church."

Stop telling the Man of God to disobey God, by expressing to him that you can take care of yourself without him! Now I see why so many families are broken. Yes, a part of the reason is that women do not want to be cared for by men! Wow!

Please do not be mad at me, I am trying to help us. A few women are always trying to show a man she is more than capable of handling business alone. Just maybe he is waiting his turn to show you that he has it!

You are able to carry yourself but he is strong enough to carry you both! Give the man of God a chance.

Yes, your mother raised you to be independent. So in other words, she raised you to be alone!

Are you comfortable yet?

Speaking of being comfortable, have you made him comfortable lately? Yes, with you. If he does not find comfort in you, trust me he will find it with someone else. I can openly say that I have been with a married man. Am I proud of it? No. Most of them say, I cannot talk to her.

Yes, I am aware of the deceit of a man. Remember, we are reading on the deception of others. But seriously, please hear me. He should be more comfortable with you than anyone else, besides God.

This explains why a man leaves his father and mother to be joined with his wife and the two are united as one.

To make him comfortable is to make him relaxed, untroubled, and satisfied.

I will not complicate this message, because I want us to get it.

I hope you realize, I am being taught through the preparation of this message. There are things that come up in my Spirit that makes me say, "Ouch!" Unfortunately, I have realized I did it wrong for years while thinking I was doing it all right.

"When you know better you do better", says Bishop Dale C. Bronner.

During the time of negotiation, Tamar stated, "What will you give me so I can make sure you will keep your promise to me?" Judah said "What do you want?" Tamar named it and he gave it.

She was not afraid to say what she wanted. *You have not because you ask not.*

For years, I would not ask a man for anything. One reason is because in my first relationship, I did not have to ask for anything. He made sure I had everything, without me asking. I saw the same thing in my mother and father's relationship.

My mother was aware of where he kept his money and if she needed something she was able to use it. Does that mean she never asked my dad for anything? No.

A man can only supply the needs that he is aware of, but your unknown wants must be requested by you. Tamar made it known that she wanted something from Judah as collateral? She requested what she wanted and he gave it to her.

Do not be afraid to ask for what you want. The most that could happen is that he ends up giving you more. This should put a smile on your face. This is what your husband wants to do; keep you smiling.

I once had a problem with accepting from a man. Now how sick was that? I am serious. He would give me money and I would thank him, insist that I was okay, and then give it back to him. He was offended and he never accepted it back.

I did not understand why he was offended, but as I matured I understood. A man wants to give to his woman.

When you ask and he gives, appreciate him and show your gratitude. Express your appreciation with words. Give him a hug and a kiss. But collect it proudly. If you do not need it, put it up for a time you will need it.

Tamar did not need the collaterals at the time she asked for them, but she needed them in the future. *Wise women prepare for the future.*

She felt secure after he gave her what she asked for and wanted. In other words, she sensed safety. It is nothing like the safety of your husband. It feels good when your man has your back. And him meeting her needs, assured her that he would do what it took to keep her safe.

I hate to keep addressing this from a money stand point, but I am sure we can all relate.

I remember years ago when I was engaged, he and I were having hard times. But at night when the lights went out, he wanted sex. I could not understand how he could ask me for sex without us knowing how the Georgia Power bill was going to get paid. One day I told him, "Look I am not having sex until my bills are paid! I am not able to perform well not knowing if I will be in the dark tomorrow."

The next day, he went and got the money for the bill. And yes, I performed very well that night! Why? Because I knew I was safe for another thirty days. So I am really able to relate with Tamar.

Yes, after the bill was paid or the money was in my hand for the bill, I LET HIM HAVE SEX WITH ME!

Then purpose was fulfilled. He wanted sex and I needed the bill paid. Bill paid, lights out, and action!

Mission accomplished and we go back to business as usual!

Yes Lord, that was one of the best nights we ever had. Beloved, are you understanding the teachings of Tamar?

Now that you know them, study them to show yourself approved. These are not my teachings, this is bible based teaching for those that are saying, "And she has the nerve to profess herself as a Christian." I am a Christian. But the difference is that I am a Spiritual Believer, not religious by any means.

I just have to straighten the way for those that might be walking sideways.

Are you still here? Hopefully, you are.

4

Judah's Lessons

1. He mourned.

2. He supervised.

3. He noticed her.

4. He stopped and propositioned her.

5. He answered her.

6. He made her a promise.

7. He was questioned by her.

8. He heard her request.

9. He gave what she requested.

10. He was liberated by her.

11. He got her pregnant.

12. He admitted they were his.

Woman of God there is much we can learn from this story. I have broken it down into layers and I am about to bring it all together.

Did I say thanks for purchasing this book? Thank you so much, because this is a powerful Word of God. It will not only show you how to relate to a man, but it will show you how powerful you are!

If you know there is a gift on the inside of your man that needs to be birth through you, will you pout because he has not yet released it? No, I will tell you what you will do.

First, let us examine ourselves. Let us make sure we are not wicked or doing wicked things that may be hindering the vision of God, that's has been placed in the Man of God. His vision was designed to be delivered through us.

Are you a wicked Woman in the sight of God? Are you doing evil things to the man of God or in God's sight? We must ask ourselves these questions too. Oftentimes, he is trying to connect with you but he cannot. Why not?

Because you think it's all about you. You are not concerned about anything he has going on, because you have so many plans for yourself. Plans he has no part of! So please check yourself.

Though Judah is a man, there is a lot that women can learn from him. So take notes. I have listed a few questions for you to ponder on.

Whenever a question is asked, it makes you aware of things that you may need to stop doing, start doing, or change. In making a change you will stop one thing and start another. Because to change a bad habit, you must discontinue the bad practice and begin a new one.

1. Have you mourned your loss? Sister, if you lost something in the past that you have not yet grieved, I give you permission to do so now. Because not experiencing the grieving process, can hinder his vision and your purpose.

2. Are you afraid? Has someone told you that you will never give birth? Did someone say that you will not be a good parent because you weren't parented well? Or, can this be something you are telling yourself? Fear not! With God with you, who can be against you? It would not matter because He is all you need.

3. What are you trying to protect from death? What or who do you care so much for that you are not willing to give, because you are scared it will die? Could it be that you are not allowing it to prosper? By you refusing to release it, you are causing death upon it.

4. Do you allow the man of God the chance to answer the questions you have asked him? Or do you answer for him? I am onto something now, I can feel it! Give him time to respond.

5. Are you willing to receive him or receive from him? I cannot stress this enough, please allow the Man of God to impart into you because he has much to give.

6. Can he be liberated through you? To help someone get free is as rewarding as being freed.

7. Will you carry, nurture, and bring forth his vision? Can he trust you with his vision?

8. Will you let him admit he is wrong? Or will you admit he is right? Can you admit you are wrong? If he admits he is wrong, he is indirectly saying you are right. We must learn to read the fine print. I am helping somebody today.

9. Are you living up to God or the reputation of the world? Everyone has a reputation to protect.

10. Are you being deceptive? If you are deceiving the Man of God, you're deceiving yourself! Judah deceive Tamar, but then Tamar deceived him. You see how his deception, in turn, deceived him.

I was once mislead and I have misdirected others as well. But my story did not end the way Judah's and Tamar's did. Let me share briefly.

I was going out on dates with a guy that I was attracted to. I openly shared every thought and feeling I had for and towards him. He was aware that I am a mother of three and a grandmother of two. He knew this about me before he asked me out. He had no intentions on being with a woman that had children, but he never shared this news with me.

For months we went out and spent time with one another, getting my feelings and emotions even more entangled with him. Then, one day he decided to share this information with me. He said, "I want my OWN family!" I asked him, "Are you saying you do not want a woman with children?" He responded, "Yes. I am sorry, but that is what I am saying." At that point, I asked myself why he would have entertained me for this long? DECEPTION!

Is your marriage built on a lie? If so, tear it down and rebuild it!

Queen, do not be dishonest with the King. Always tell him the truth. *The truth shall make you free!*

And never let him find out the truth through someone else! Never. This can be dangerous!

Have you noticed how important you are to God and to the man of God? God created women from men, but now men are created through women.

God is entrusting you with something so precious, the Gift of Life to be born through you.

Your request was known to God and with that request being granted, it gives you the responsibility to your husband and his vision. Are you prepared to manage it properly, by not aborting it with any past hurt and/or anger, moving forward?

If so, meet me in chapter five where it comes alive!

5

A Word from the Lord

I *have* *poured* the foundation and built the house, so now let's decorate it. I know women love to decorate their new houses.

Romans 12:2

Don't copy the behavior and the customs of the world, but let God transform you into a new person by changing the way you think. Then you will know what God wants you to do, you will know how good and pleasing and perfect his will is.

Isaiah 43:19

For I am about to do a brand new thing. See, I have already begun! Do you see it? I will make a pathway through the wilderness for my people to come home. I will create rivers for them in the desert.

I am so excited about the new thing God is doing in the lives of his people. Men, women, girls, and boys both young and old.

People have been waiting on a change and you may be one of those people. I am speaking this word as God spoke it to me and through me. But confirmation was through my Bishop Dale C. Bronner.

God spoke to me as clear as you are reading the words off of these pages. He said to me, "There is a *Unique Shift* taking place in the body of Christ. You will know longer think the same and/or do things the same. Your actions and reactions will not remain the same."

This shift is much different from any other shift that has taken place before. See, some shifts take you from one grade level to the next. But this shift is taking some from elementary to middle, middle to high school, high school to college. In some cases, the *Unique Shift* God has in place has already taken place and has had others to be SKIPPED! You won't go through the same channels as others.

This shift is not just a promotional shift beloved! This *Unique Shift*, was designed and orchestrated by God. He is doing things in the lives of His people that no man can or will take credit for In the Mighty Name of Jesus!

Woman of God, do you believe in Miracles, Signs, and Wonders?

Mark 16:15-18

And then he told them, "Go into all the world and preach the Good News to everyone, everywhere. Anyone who believes and is baptized will be saved. But anyone who refuses to believe will be condemned. These will accompany those who believe: They will cast out demons in my name, and they will speak new languages. They will be able to handle snakes with safety, and if they drink anything poisonous, it won't hurt them. They will be able to place their hands on the sick and heal them.

Woman of God, I speak to your Spirit in Jesus' Name.

Today is the day that the Lord has made, you shall rejoice and be glad therein it. Weeping may endure for a night but Joy comes in the morning light.

At this moment, I will prophesy to the dry bones that they shall live again In Jesus' Name Amen!

Woman of God, I need you to Shift your thoughts in the Mighty Name of Jesus. Shift your sight in Jesus' Name. Shift your hearing ability in Jesus' Name Amen. Shift your senses in Jesus' Name. Shift your taste buds in Jesus' Name. Amen!

Philippians 4:8

And now dear brothers and sisters, let me say one more thing as I close this letter. Fix your thoughts on what is true and honorable and right. Think about things that are pure and lovely and admirable. Think about things that are excellent and worthy of praise.

Colossians 3:1-2

1Since you have been raised to new life with Christ, set your sights on the realities of heaven, where Christ sits at God's right hand in the place of honor and power. 2Let heaven fill your thoughts. Do not think only about things down here on earth.

John 10:27

My sheep recognize my voice; I know them and they know me.

Psalm 34:8

Taste and see that the Lord is good. Oh, the joys of those who trust in him!

Woman of God, I do not think I need to say anything else. Expect God to do something brand new in your life, in the man of God, and in the relationship between the two of you.

If God has not been the center of your relationship, please invite Him.

Ecclesiastes 4:12

A person standing alone can be attacked and defeated, but two can stand back to back and conquer. Three are even better, for a triple braided cord is not easily broken.

I pray your spiritual ears are in tune with the Holy Spirit, because this is none of me and all of God.

May God bless you richly!

6

In My Own Words

Er was wicked and Onan did a wicked thing in God's sight.

Who are you and what are you doing in God's sight?

Will it put you to death?

He told her to return home to her parents, stay a widow, and he would send for her when his son was old enough to marry. But that was not what he intended to do.

This is when the deception began. He deceived her first.

Who have you swindled lately?

Then, Tamar got word!

She then took off the old garments and put on the new clothes. She dressed for the occasion; it was time to handle her business.

She went and waited, but she knew two things that were working in her favor.

One, he was sexually frustrated due to his wife being deceased. And two, she was looking too good for him not to notice her.

Right timing. Timing is everything! He noticed her, stopped, and propositioned her.

She appeared to be a prostitute in his sight. Meaning his vision was not clear. But she did not respond to him angrily, when he offered her money for sex. One, she knew she was not a prostitute. Two, she knew it was a gift in him to make boys because he once had three sons.

She recognized it was purpose in him, that needed to be transferred into her. Guess what? The purpose was more valuable than who he thought she was.

She was not a bit bothered about how he viewed her outer appearance, because she was more concerned about his inner appearance (potential).

But she needed collateral to keep her alive. Sometimes we know if we get caught, we can get a life sentence or the death penalty. But if we have a witness or some form of proof, we may be exonerated.

She needed proof. She did not care about the initial promise (the young goat). That was just a part of the negotiation.

Sometimes when signing an agreement, there are things in the contract that really does not matter.

Have you ever made a deal with someone and they gave you something extra, for free, if you joined that day? But in actuality, you had no use of it. Tamar did not want a goat. She needed verification that they had slept together, because she was fertile. It was her time of ovulation and tonight she was planning on conceiving by Judah!

It reminds me of when Ruth went and laid at Boaz's feet. *Naomi said, "Don't worry daughter, he will make good on this tonight!"*

Tamar knew that night she was getting pregnant with his vision and she would need the DNA results before the delivery, so he could spare her life!

After she negotiated and reached an agreement, she requested what she wanted. He in return gave it to her. Then, she let him sleep with her. Not fighting him off saying, "I am tired. Not tonight. Never mind. Maybe we can, next time."

She gave of herself, so she could receive the purpose that was in him. She put herself in a receiving position, as well.

A lot of women know how to give, but they do not know how to receive! Open yourself up to receive.

Give and it shall be given. To the measure you give, is the measure you shall receive. Many of you, shall get pregnant TONIGHT!

Are you excited?

Do you realize Tamar talked to no one? Woman of God, listen to me. Do not talk to anyone about anything. Go before God right now, trusting that whatever you are desiring to get pregnant with will be conceived. Tonight is the night!

This may be your night to get pregnant, your night to toil the soil, and/or become fertile. But tonight, this word is preparing you to open yourself to receive the anointing of the Holy Spirit; to birth what was once called potential!

After Tamar got pregnant, she went home and continued to handle business as usual. Just because you are expecting, does not mean you are dismissed from other responsibilities. Please make a note of this!

She put up her sword. You will need this very soon.

Say out loud, "In three months!" In three months your husband will get word that you are pregnant with a gift. He will be furious! He may say things like, "We cannot afford another child, or a child at all. How?

We have tried for years and now of all times. We are not able to leave our jobs and start a business or ministry. How can we work and do ministry full-time?"

That is when you pull out your sword (ammunition) and say, "Do you remember when you said that you wanted to start the tire shop?...Well I began visualizing you running it. I thought of a name for it, picked out the location, and purchased the business license. Today it is all yours. Do you remember discussing this with me?"

He will look at the vision and respond, "Yes! This belongs to me; it's mine! I admit, I shared my vision with you and you ran with the vision!"

In due season, the opening day will give birth. Not to just one, but two! God will give him back what he lost, but he will give you double the trouble. *"So get ready, get ready; get ready!", in my TD Jakes voice.*

The time to be ready; is not the time to get ready! - Bishop Dale C. Bronner.

As Tamar was giving birth, the midwife put the scarlet onto what appeared to be the first born's wrist. But the second child, named Perez, came first. BREAKING THROUGH!

In order for the midwife to have the scarlet prepared to be put on the first born, they had to have known it was two before her delivery date. Someone did an ultrasound!

The ultrasound read, "Woman of God. My child, I blessed your womb to give birth to two sons! You only asked for one, but you gave of yourself twice and never conceived anything. As a result of it, in due season you shall bring forth two ministries, two businesses, and two children. One named BREAKTHROUGH and the other named ARISE!"

THIS IS YOUR BREAKTHROUGH SEASON AND YOU SHALL ARISE NOW IN JESUS' NAME!

Let this word begin to penetrate through your heart and allow God to put His super to your natural. Causing a Supernatural Blessing to override your deception, bringing forth the Blessing of God!

The potential gift, when birthed out, becomes the blessing of God.

While studying the word potential, I realized the first six letters reads *potent*.

> *Potent is having great power, influence, or effect.*

I pray the potency of this message revives and revolutionizes your very being, so that you spring forth in your prosperity In Jesus' Name Amen!

7

Scriptures Just For You

1 Samuel 15:22

22But Samuel replied, "What is more pleasing to the Lord: your burnt offerings and sacrifice. Listening to him is much better than offering the fat of rams.

Ephesians 5:22

22You wives will submit to your husbands as you do to the Lord.

Ephesians 4:24

24You must display a new nature because you are a new person, created in God's likeness – righteous, holy, and true.

1 Corinthians 11:7

7For a man ought not to have his head covered, since he is the image and glory of God; but the woman is the glory of man.

Psalms 27:14

14Wait patiently for the Lord. Be brave and courageous. Yes, wait patiently for the Lord.

Luke 11:9

9And so I tell you, keep on asking, and you will be given what you ask for. Keep on looking and you will find. Keep on knocking and the door will be open. For everyone who asks, receives. Everyone who seeks, finds. And the door is opened to everyone who knocks.

2 Corinthians 1: 3-4

3All praise to the God and Father of our Lord Jesus Christ. He is the source* of every mercy and the God who comforts us. 4He comforts us all in our troubles so that we can comfort others. When others are troubled, we will be able to give them the same comfort God has given us.

Proverbs 27:13

13Be sure to get collateral from anyone who guarantees the debt of a stranger. Get a deposit if someone guarantees the debt of an adulterous woman.

Psalms 91:4

14He will shield you with his feathers. His faithful promises are your armor and protection.

Matthew 5:16

16In the same way, let your good deeds shine out for all to see, so that everyone will praise your heavenly Father.

Jeremiah 29:11

11For I know the plans I have for you, says the Lord. They are plans for good and not for disaster, to give you a future and a hope.

Matthew 25:21

21The master was full of praise. Well done my good and faithful servant. You have been faithful in handling this small amount, so now I will give you many more responsibilities. Let's celebrate together!

His breakthrough is through you!   His vision is your mission!

And you shall receive DOUBLE, In Jesus' Name Amen!

For that reason, I need you to see and treat yourself differently. Then, He will do the same.

People do not treat you the way you treat them; they treat you the way you treat yourself. - Shakisha Edness.

Now it's time for you to labor in Prayer, Praise, and Worship; as if you know God is going to bless through you, In Jesus' Name Amen!

It's your birthing season. Give birth to your ministry, business, or vision NOW!

Below are definitions of words that are discussed during the seven chapters of this book. Read and study them.

Break through is an important finding.

Break is to breach or fracture, a stopping or pause, a sudden move, to split, come apart, to become inoperable, to sever relationships, to appear or happen suddenly, to run away, to part by force, to ruin or cause to fail, to violate the terms of a contract.

Through is to complete, done and finish.

Condoms is a thin rubber sheath worn on a man's penis during sexual intercourse as a contraceptive and/or as protection against infection. The deliberate use of artificial methods or other techniques to prevent pregnancy as a consequence of sexual intercourse.

Use is the act of using or the state of being used. The purpose for which something is used.

Wear is to have on the person, as a garment or ornament; to display, as an aspect; to damage by constant use, to exhaust. To be diminished by use, to withstand the effects of use, time, etc. To have a tiring effect. The act of wearing or being worn; articles of dress, destruction from use or time, durability.

Wicked is evil, mischievous, or roguish; mean or troublesome.

Obey is to accept or follow.

Disguise is that used to conceal the identity of a person or thing. To alter or conceal the identity of, to misrepresent.

Veil is a thin fabric for covering the face; anything that conceals or covers. To cover, conceal and disguise.

Wait is to anticipate; to pause; to delay; to remain in readiness. To remain in expectation of.

Question is an inquiry; something open to discussion. To ask.

Comfortable is to be at ease; free from pain or stress; adequate.

Negotiate is to confer in an attempt to reach agreement. To compromise or agree, as to price, terms, etc. To transfer ownership, as of security.

Collect is to gather; to secure payment.

Collaterals are similar; of a thing pledged as a guarantee for fulfillment of an obligation. That pledged as a guarantee.

Secure is too unlikely to the threatened or overcome. To protect; to make certain; to obtain.

Let is to permit or allow.

Purpose is an aim or goal. An intention.

Accomplish is to complete. Fulfill. Proficient.

Potential is having the capacity to become or develop into something in the future.

Birth is the emergence of a baby or other young from the body of its mother; the start of life as a physical separate being.

Blessing is having God's favor and protection.

Potent is Powerful, Strong, Mighty, formidable, influential, dominant and forceful.

Below are very important characters that are discussed previously, and the meaning of their names.

Kezib *is a place in the plain of Judah.*

Tamar *the 'date palm tree'.*

Judah *is one who 'give praise to God'.*

Er *spelled backwards, in Hebrew, is the word evil.*

Onan *is 'the virile one'.*

Perez *is he who pushes through.*

The one who breaks through a wall.

Zerah *is he who arise.*

About The Author

SHAKISHA SHAMAIN EDNESS, a writer, mentor, motivational speaker, and evangelist for Christ. Speaking Truth, Changing Perception, and Gaining Lives to Christ by sharing her testimonies and word of God. She is from Newark, New Jersey and partially raised in Atlanta, Georgia. She found her passion through her pain and her pain then directed her to her God's given purpose. She is truly an inspiration to others and she gives all the recognition to Jesus!

Shakisha Edness is the CEO/Founder of TRA-C Inc., which is named after her beloved mother Tracie. TRA-C Inc. was founded in 2006. A nonprofit organization that is designed to educate and empower men, women, and children that are affected directly and indirectly by HIV/AIDS and drug/alcohol abuse. She has mentored men in Atlanta group homes sharing her testimonies and have mentored the youth of Paulding County Public School System.

She is also the CEO/Founder of Women Overcoming Weight-loss, which has touched the lives of many women, since it was founded in 2009. She ministers to women on a daily basis through a conference call prayer line, where she has seen blessings and miracles take place in many lives.

Shakisha became an Adolescent Peer Counselor under Sandra Mc Donald, the Founder of Outreach, Inc. Working side by side with her mother at age fifteen, sharing her story of an addict's child. Shakisha since then has pursued her career in motivational speaking, evangelizing, and writing to minister to those she may never get a chance to meet.

Shakisha is an extension of God's love without limits.

AUTHOR CONTACT

INFORMATION

To purchase books, for more information, or to schedule
Shakisha Edness to speak, please contact:

Shakisha Edness

www.shakishaedness.com

UPCOMING BOOKS BY
SHAKISHA SHAMAIN EDNESS

Break Through Volume II
Break Through I & II Workbook
Women Overcoming Weight-loss Book
Women Overcoming Weight-loss Journal
Women Overcoming Weight-loss Workbook
Uncovering Me through Poetry
A Christmas to Remember
From the Eyes of a Child
A Man Can Only Do What a Woman Allows

.

www.ingramcontent.com/pod-product-compliance
Lightning Source LLC
LaVergne TN
LVHW051816080426
835513LV00017B/1981